AUSTRALIA AND NEW ZEALAND

A TRUE BOOK

by

Elaine Landau

Children's Press®

A Division of Grolier Publishing

New York London Hong Kong Sydney
Danbury, Connecticut

Reading Consultant
Linda Cornwell
*Coordinator of School Quality
and Professional Improvement
Indiana State Teachers
Association*

Author's Dedication
For Michael

An Australian black swan

Visit Children's Press® on the
Internet at:
http://publishing.grolier.com

Library of Congress Cataloging-in-Publication Data

Landau, Elaine.
    Australia and New Zealand / by Elaine Landau.
        p.   cm. — (A true book)
    Includes bibliographical references and index.
    Summary: Discusses the history, geography, people, government, and
economy of Australia and New Zealand.
    ISBN: 0-516-20981-7 (lib. bdg.)   0-516-26573-3 (pbk.)
    1. Australia—Juvenile literature. 2. New Zealand—Juvenile literature.
[1. Australia. 2. New Zealand.] I. Title. II. Series.
DU96.L36   1999
994—dc21   98-50881
                                                            CIP
                                                            AC

GROLIER
PUBLISHING

Contents

This coastal area of Queensland, Australia, is well populated.

Australia and New Zealand

Australia is both a country and a continent. It is the world's sixth-largest nation and its smallest continent. Australia includes the island of Tasmania to the south of the continent, and some smaller nearby islands. Lying between the Indian and Pacific oceans,

A view of south Australia's desert region

Australia is completely surrounded by water.

Much of the Australian continent is desert. Few people live in these areas. Only a few coastal places receive enough rainfall for large numbers of people to live comfortably. Two such areas are Australia's northeast and southeast coasts.

The nation of New Zealand lies about 1,500 miles (2,400 kilometers) southeast of Australia. It is also surrounded by water. Located in the southwestern Pacific Ocean, it consists of two large islands. They are North Island and South Island. There are numerous smaller islands, as

South Island is the home of 12,349-foot (3,764-meter)-high Mt. Cook, New Zealand's highest mountain.

well. New Zealand's South Island is quite mountainous. Its North Island has fewer mountains and most of the nation's people.

New Zealand is known for its beauty. There are mountain

ranges, lush forests, water-
falls, and lovely harbors and
beaches.

Australia's weather is mostly warm and dry. However, the
climate varies in different
areas of the country. Part of
Australia lies in the Tropics,
where it is usually hot all year
round. The rest of the country
is cooler with warm summers
and mild winters.

New Zealand has a mild
and moist climate. Rainfall is

plentiful. Yet there is a lot of sunshine, too. Summer temperatures usually range from about 68 to 77 degrees Fahrenheit (20 to 25 degrees Celsius). Winter temperatures are usually from about 50 to 60 degrees Fahrenheit (10 to 15 degrees Celsius). New Zealand's climate also varies in different parts of the country. South Island is cooler than North Island.

New Zealand and Australia lie south of the equator. As a

This summer-time view of Sydney, Australia, was photographed during the month of January.

result, seasons there are opposite of seasons in countries lying north of the equator. Winter is from June to September. Summer is from December to March.

NEW ZEALAND

NORTH ISLAND

● Auckland

Waikato River

INDIAN OCEAN

☆ Wellington

Cook Strait

SOUTHERN ALPS

▲ Mt. Cook

● Christchurch

Waitaki River

PACIFIC OCEAN

SOUTH ISLAND

Clutha River

● Dunedin

Stewart Island

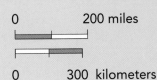

0   200 miles

0   300 kilometers

The People

More than eighteen million
people live in Australia.
About three and a half million
people live in New Zealand.
Most have British origins.

After World War II
(1939–45), many Italians,
Greeks, and Germans settled
in Australia. More recently,

Most Australians and New Zealanders have British origins.

increasing numbers of Asians have settled there. Many of the people settling in New Zealand are from Great Britain, Australia, and the Netherlands.

Other ethnic groups living in New Zealand and Australia are

This Maori woman and child are wearing traditional clothing.

the native people who were there before the Europeans arrived. The Maori, who went to New Zealand from islands in the South Pacific more than one thousand years ago, were its early inhabitants.

The Aboriginals lived in Australia before the Europeans arrived. They hunted, fished, and gathered food. Much of their culture and way of life

Aboriginals have lived in Australia for more than 40,000 years.

did not survive the Europeans' arrival. Today Aboriginals make up only a small portion of Australia's population.

Most Australians and New Zealanders speak English. The native people of both countries speak their own language. Many also speak English.

Food in Australia and New Zealand is similar. In both countries, beef, lamb, and mutton are favorites.

A skiier in the mountains of New Zealand's South Island

Sports and outdoor activities are popular in both nations. Australians enjoy water sports, cricket (similar to baseball), rugby (similar to football) and soccer. New Zealanders also like cricket and rugby, as well as water sports, hiking, skiing, and ice hockey.

This student is schooled from his home in a remote area of Australia.

In Australia, students must attend school from age six to fifteen. New Zealanders must attend school from age five through fifteen.

Australian students who live in out-of-the-way areas can be instructed through government-sponsored radio transmissions. Students and teachers communicate through two-way radios. Homework and tests are sent through the mail.

The people of New Zealand and Australia have long been active in the arts. Beautiful Maori wood carvings and Aboriginal art are displayed in museums and art galleries in

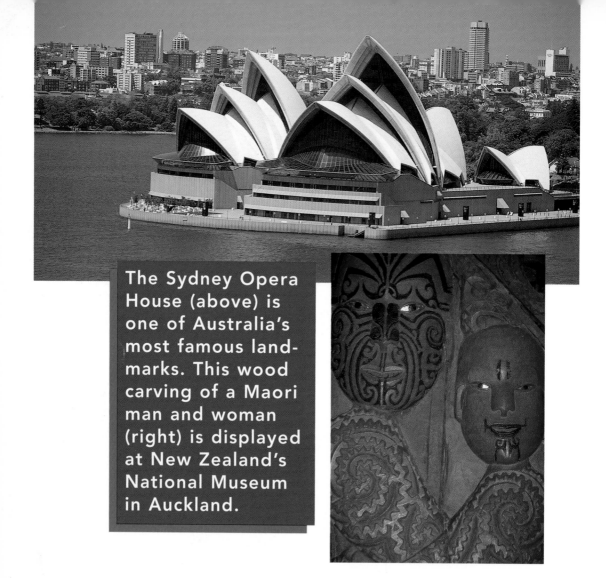

The Sydney Opera House (above) is one of Australia's most famous landmarks. This wood carving of a Maori man and woman (right) is displayed at New Zealand's National Museum in Auckland.

New Zealand and Australia. Opera and theater are also popular in both countries.

Quick Facts About Australia

Official Name: Commonwealth of Australia

Head of Government: Prime Minister

Area: 2,978,147 square miles (7,713,364 square kilometers)

Capital: Canberra

Largest Cities: Sydney, Melbourne, Brisbane, Perth, Adelaide

Major Language: English

Major Religions: Protestant, Roman Catholic

Schoolchildren in a park near Adelaide, Australia

The Australian flag

History of Two Nations

Throughout the 1500s and 1600s, Portuguese, Spanish, and Dutch explorers landed in Australia. But they found only dry land that looked as if nothing could grow. So they did not start permanent settlements.

In 1770, Captain James Cook of Great Britain's Royal Navy

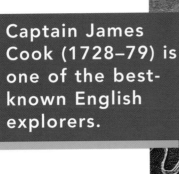

Captain James Cook (1728–79) is one of the best-known English explorers.

landed on Australia's east coast. The land there was good for growing crops. He named the area New South Wales.

In 1788, a British prison population of more than one thousand people, including guards and their families, was established in New South Wales. As time passed, the British started additional colonies in other parts of Australia.

Once there were more free settlers than prisoners, a movement for independence grew. By the 1890s, the people wanted to become an independent nation. On January 1, 1901, the Australian colonies officially became known as the Commonwealth of Australia.

This portrait of Abel Janszoon Tasman, with his wife and daughter, was painted in 1637.

New Zealand's history is similar to Australia's. Like the Aboriginals, the Maori lived by farming, hunting, and fishing before the Europeans arrived. The first Europeans in New Zealand were a Dutch ship captain named Abel Janszoon

Tasman and his crew. They landed in 1642, but left after being attacked by the Maori. In 1769, a year before he arrived in Australia, Captain Cook landed in New Zealand. Cook made friends with the Maori and mapped the area.

During the next thirty years, New Zealand drew hunters and traders from England, France, and the United States. Released prisoners from Australia also arrived. Some—mostly the British—stayed and became the country's first colonists. They raised sheep, grew wheat, and mined for gold.

Eventually, Great Britain established its rule. But by the early 1900s, New Zealanders wanted more independence. Today, New Zealand has its own government, but it remains a part of Great Britain.

The Governments

Australia has a government in which the leader of the country is called the prime minister. The main lawmaking body is called the Parliament. But Australia is also a constitutional monarchy. This means that Great Britain's king or queen is the ruler of Australia. However,

Australia's old (foreground) and new (background) Parliament buildings are located in Canberra.

as in Great Britain, royalty has no real power in the day-to-day governing of the country.

New Zealand's Parliament building in Wellington, the nation's capital

Like Australia, New Zealand is a constitutional monarchy. It also has a prime minister and a Parliament. The prime minister and the Parliament are responsible for governing the country.

Quick Facts About New Zealand

Official Name: New Zealand

Head of Government: Prime Minister

Area: About 103,884 square miles (About 270,534 square kilometers)

Capital: Wellington

Largest Cities: Auckland, Christchurch, Dunedin

Major Language: English

Major Religions Church of England, Methodist, Presbyterian, Roman Catholic

Maori and white school-children perform a traditional Maori dance.

New Zealand's flag

The Nations' Economies

Australia is a prosperous nation partly because of its mining and farming industries. Each year, its exports include: copper, gold, silver, coal, uranium, natural gas, and petroleum (oil). Australia is also the world's largest producer of precious gems such as diamonds and opals.

Part of Australia is farmland. Wheat, barley, oats, cotton, rice, fruits, and sugarcane are grown on the coastal regions of Australia's east, southeast, and southwest. Most of Australia's farmland is grazing area for the large number of sheep and cattle raised there. The nation exports great amounts of beef and dairy products. Australia is also the world's biggest wool exporter.

Much of New Zealand's wealth comes from farming. New Zealand exports large quantities of butter, cheese, meat, and wool. (Although there are only three and a half million people, there are more than sixty-seven million sheep!)

A sheep's wool is removed by a process called shearing.

Recently, manufacturing has grown in New Zealand.

Tourism also provides another source of money for both New Zealand and Australia.

Unique Wildlife and Sights

Australia and New Zealand are home to some animals that can not be found anywhere else. Australia has many members of the kangaroo family—ranging from the 16-inch (41-centimeter)-long rat kangaroo to the 6-foot (183-cm)-tall red kangaroo.

Some of Australia's best-known animals include (clockwise from top left): the red kangaroo, koala, echidna, tiger snake, and platypus.

Another well-known animal is the koala, a furry creature that looks similar to a teddy bear.

Other unusual Australian animals include the platypus and the echidna. These are the only mammals on Earth that do not give birth to live young. Instead, their offspring hatch from eggs.

Australia is also home to rare black swans and the poisonous tiger snake—one of the deadliest snakes in the world.

Another of Australia's special features is the Great Barrier Reef. Found along the northeast coast, it is 1,250 miles

A small plane carries sightseers over the Great Barrier Reef.

(2,012 km) long. It is the largest coral reef on Earth.

New Zealand also has unique animals. It is home to a mini-dinosaur known as the tuatara. This small prehistoric-looking reptile died out every-where else more than one

The tuatara (top) and the kakopo (above) can be found only in New Zealand. A visitor looks tiny next to the world's largest kauri tree (left). These huge trees can grow up to 275 feet (84 meters) tall.

hundred million years ago. The kakopo is the world's largest and only flightless parrot.

New Zealand has many striking features including volcanoes, glaciers, geysers, and hot springs. Its huge kauri trees can live as long as one thousand years.

Australia's and New Zealand's interesting history, beautiful scenery, and unique wildlife have attracted visitors for many years. Both countries face a bright, prosperous future.

To Find Out More

Here are some additional resources to help you learn more about the nations of Australia and New Zealand:

 **Books**

Allison, Robert J. **Australia.** Raintree Steck-Vaughn, 1996.

Brady, Peter. **Sheep.** Capstone Press, 1996.

Cousteau Society. **An Adventure In New Zealand.** Simon & Schuster Books For Young Readers, 1992.

Jansen, John. **Playing Possum: Riddles about Kangaroos, Koalas, and Other Marsupials.** Lerner Publications, 1995.

Lee, Sandra. **Koalas.** Child's World, Inc., 1993.

Nile, Richard. **Australian Aborigines.** Raintree Steck-Vaughn, 1993.

Petersen, David. **Australia.** Children's Press, 1998.

Organizations and Online Sites

About Australia
http://www.about-australia
.com

Learn what it's like in each of Australia's states and territories: news, sports, weather, attractions, museums, education, travel tips, and more.

Great Barrier Reef Aquarium
http://www.aquarium.org.au/

Real-time pictures from inside the aquarium, plus a lot of photos, maps, links, and a "living classroom."

New Zealand.com
http://nz.com/

Take a virtual tour, send an electronic postcard, and learn all about New Zealand.

Parliament of Australia
http://www.aph.gov.au/
parl.htm

Learn about Australia's constitution, prime minister, senate, house of representatives, and much more.

Passport to New Zealand
http://www.nztb.govt.nz/

Visitor information, facts about New Zealand, links to other sites, and current and upcoming events.

New Zealand Tourism Board
780 3rd Ave.
Suite 1904
New York, NY 10017-2024

Important Words

climate the usual weather in a place

continent one of the seven great land masses of Earth

export to send products to other countries for sale

inhabitant someone who lives in a specific place or area

mammals warm-blooded animals with backbones that nurse their young, examples include: humans, dogs, mice, and kangaroos

mutton meat from a sheep

prosperous successful, wealthy

unique special, unlike anything else

Index

Meet the Author

Elaine Landau has a Bachelor of Arts degree in English and Journalism from New York University and a Masters degree in Library and Information Science from Pratt Institute. She has worked as a newspaper reporter, children's book editor, and a youth services librarian, but especially enjoys writing for young people.

Ms. Landau has written more than one hundred nonfiction books on various topics. She lives in Miami, Florida, with her husband Norman and son, Michael.